MINISTERS OF GRACE
The Unauthorized Shakespearean Parody of Ghostbusters

By

Jordan Monsell

Inspired by the work of
Dan Aykroyd, Harold Ramis,
and
William Shakespeare

Shadowcut Press
Los Angeles

Shadowcut Press
5325 Radford Ave. #8
Valley Village, CA 91607

ISBN:1544804784
ISBN:9781544804781

For Mom,
from her little Ghostbuster

MINISTERS
of
RACE

DRAMATIS PERSONAE

DOCTOR PETER VENKMAN
SIR RAY
LADY DANA
SIR EGON
LOUIS, a fool
JANINE, employed by the Ministers
PECK, servant to the King
SIR WINSTON
LORD MAYOR
MALE STUDENT
FEMALE STUDENT
GOZER, a traveler and demon
SLIMER, a ghost
INNKEEPER
ALICE, a book maid
GHOST OF A BOOK MAID
LANDHOLDER
CHANCELLOR
VIOLINIST
LIBRARY ADMINISTRATOR
ARCHBISHOP OF CANTERBERY
CHORUS

GUARDS, ATTENDANTS, COACHMEN, HERALDS,
MESSENGERS, MAIDS, SERVANTS, and GHOSTS

*Map of London produced during the time of Shakespeare
(1564 – 1616)*

MINISTERS OF GRACE
ACT I

ACT 1

SCENE 1

A room at Cambridge University.
Enter Dr. PETER VENKMAN, and two STUDENTS.
They sit at a table.

PETER
Now harken to my words and answer them
Contemplate upon this piece of parchment
And reveal to me what symbol 'pon it.

MALE STUDENT
Is't a square?

PETER
A valiant effort my friend, but nay.

He scalds him with hot poker.

Weed your better judgments. What read this?

JENNIFER
Be it a star?

PETER
Ay, the brightest star in all of heaven.

Now think on it.

MALE STUDENT
If it be a sphere, may I take my leave?

PETER
Oh, misprision in the highest degree!

[Scalds him]

Shalt thou answer anon? What be the card?

JENNIFER
Be it the sign of eight or lain on its side that of infinite
number?

PETER
Supposing it a thing impossible
Thou cannot see the cards I hold, tell truth?

JENNIFER
Nay, good my Lord!

PETER
I hope you do not mean to cheat me so.

JENNIFER
Nay, by my troth, I swear it. They do but come to me.

University of Cambridge arms.

PETER
Thy nerves are in their infancy again
And have no vigor in them.

MALE STUDENT
So they are.
My spirits, as in a dream, are all bound up.

PETER
Calm thyself. For but five and seventy more.
If thou were to divine what this card be?

MALE STUDENT
Three lines that like a river flow?

PETER
But nay!
It seems misfortune follows you this day.

MALE STUDENT
I know it. I –

[PETER scalds him.]

Hey! I grow quite weary of this game!

PETER
But didst thou not enlist? Have we not paid thee?

MALE STUDENT
Aye, before I knew what tortures lay in wait.
What dost thou hope to prove in all this?

PETER
Though think this madness, yet there is method in 't.

I have been studying the effect of pain on the powers of soothsaying.

MALE STUDENT
The effect? I shall tell thee of the effect. Or rather say, the cause of this defect,
For this effect defective's made by cause.

PETER
Then perchance my argument be correct!

MALE STUDENT
Enough, no more! Keep thy crown!
Thy game hath caused me injury and frown.

He Exits.

PETER
I shall do so!
    [To Jennifer]
Needs must you except, before excepted.
For such is the hard resentment that thine ability will provoke in the hearts of others.

JENNIFER
Think you I obtain this gift Doctor Venkman?

PETER
'Twas not by luck you answered true, madam.

Enter DR. RAYMOND STANTZ *in a flurry.*

RAY
This be it! By good fortune this be it!
Was lens for my camera obscura delivered? I have need of it.

PETER

[To Jennifer]

I cry your pardon.

[To Ray]

I am engaged here, Ray! I require more time with this subject.
Couldst thou call on me in one hour? Mayhap one and half
hour?

RAY

Good sir Peter, at forty past the hour of one within the Library
of Guildhall, did a crowd some ten in number bear witness to
an apparition floating and vaporous in nature. From twenty
metres blew it volumes from shelves with hellish winds and
so horridly did shake the disposition of a kindly book maid!

PETER

My admiration will not be seasoned.
I bid thee, make haste and report back to me.

RAY

Nay, nay, Peter. Th`affair cries haste and speed must answer
it.

PETER

Return with news —

RAY

I shall have you with us in this cause. Sir Spengler with
dowsing rods in hand, has taken' readings strange and waits
upon us even now. My own occasion peaks!

PETER

As does mine own

I must take my leave of you. But come. We shall meet again and it will be so far forth friendly maintained. Mayhap thou could return this eve, belike--

JENNIFER
Eight o' the clock?

PETER
Thou hast spoke the words I was thinking on! Eight o' the clock?
Thy powers as soothsayer are legitimate!
I shall see thee then when the cock crows eight
Send silent word through mind if you run late.

Exeunt.

Dowsing rod

SCENE 2

Guildhall Library. Enter PETER and RAY.

PETER
As thy friend, I must speak true. Thou hast gone mad with
this talk of ghosts. Running about the city holding parley with
each half a soul and notion crazed who claim they have
witnessed the supernatural. What hast thou seen but in thy
mind's eye?

RAY
There are more things in heaven and earth, Peter, than are
dreamt of in your philosophy.
Let me remember thee 'twas I who bore witness some full
fathom five the unexplained exodus of sponges.

PETER
Good cuz, said sponges moved but a foot and nail.

DR. EGON SPENGLER *is under a table, listening with a cone to
his ear. PETER speaks in a ghostly voice.*

PETER
Mark me....

EGON
Ah, we are all met.

PETER
What hast thou begot?

EGON
This is much, Sir Peter. Much indeed. There be something
present here.

PETER
Egon, I am reminded of the hour you did attempt to bore a
hole through thy costard.

EGON
'Twould have worked an thee hadn't stopped me.

Enter LIBRARY ADMINISTRATOR

LIBRARY ADMINISTRATOR
I am Roger Delicore by name. Art thou the men from
University?

PETER
The very same. I be Doctor Venkman. Doctor Stantz, Egon.

LIBRARY ADMINISTRATOR
I thank you gentlemen for your company. It is my wish that in
haste and quiet this be resolved.

PETER
Let us not stand in sudden haste. They stumble that run fast.

They go to ALICE, who lies on a table.

ALICE
Recall I not legs, but with arms outstretched, it did beckon.

RAY
Arms? To face this spirit I would not be delayed!

PETER
I wish to importune thee madam.

Hast thou or any of thy kin been lunatic?

ALICE
St. Jerome, mine uncle, thought he was.

PETER
Verily, that seemeth an affirmation.
Abuse thy delicate youth withal drugs or minerals?

ALICE
Nay good sir!

PETER
I cry thou mercy. And 'tis that time of moon with you?

LIBRARY ADMINISTRATOR
For what reason ask this, I beseech you?

PETER
Come from thy ward. I be a philosopher.

EGON
It moves, even now. We shall follow it.

Exeunt.

SCENE 3
*Guildhall Library. Cellar. Enter EGON with dowsing rods, RAY
with camera obscura, and PETER. They come to a tall tower of
books.*

RAY
Look ye!

EGON
This haste was hot in question cuz.

RAY
A well-balanced stacking of books is this. Mine eyes have not
seen the like since the bloody turbulence of Warwickshire in
the year of our Lord 1589.

PETER
Be it true. No man would volumes stack.

RAY
Hark!
What be yonder odor that infects my nostrils such?
What direful spectacle of a wrack is this?

EGON
Look ye here Raymond.

RAY
The remnants of an apparition

EGON
Venkman, I bid thee retrieve an ounce.

RAY
In nature as in name.

PETER
One discharges their nose and thou wish to keep it?

EGON
I wish to study it.
This be the path from whence discomfort swells.

RAY
Come apace.

PETER
Egon, thy discharge.

A bookshelf falls with a crash.

Such a thing befall you ere long?

They shake their heads.

Be the first?

They nod. Enter GHOST.

EGON
'Tis here.

RAY
A fine apparition, in nature as in name

PETER
Alas, what shall we do?
Prithee, woulds't thou come hither and parlay for a moment?
Cousins, a word, I pray you? What shall we do?

RAY
I know not. What think you Egon?

EGON reveals an abacus. PETER slaps it away.

PETER
Cease!

RAY
It would be spoke to. One of us shall act as deputy.

EGON
'Tis a point of wisdom.

> *They look to PETER. He groans and approaches the ghost.*

PETER
Good morrow. I am Peter called. Whence came you? Be thou a
spirit of health or goblin damn'd?
Speak. I am bound to hear.

LIBRARY GHOST
Sssssh.

PETER
'Tis not so well our converse.

RAY
Very well. A plan I have devised to confront this apparition.
Follow close behind and be content.
Anon! Have at thee!

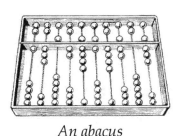

An abacus

They Exit, running. LIBRARY ADMINISTRATOR chases after.

LIBRARY ADMINISTRATOR
Did'st thou see it? What be it?

PETER
We shall withall expedient duty see you.

Exeunt.

Robert Thew (engraver) after Henry Fuseli,
Hamlet: Act I, Scene IV

SCENE 4

University Grounds. Enter PETER, RAY and EGON.

PETER
Have at thee! 'twas the extent of your plan. Have at thee. 'twas precise.

RAY
Season my admiration I did not
We did it wrong, being so majestical,
To offer it the show of violence,
For it is as the air, invulnerable,
And our vain blows malicious mockery.
Yet touched, we three, the spiritual veil
Know'est what this could mean to the academe?

PETER
Aye. 'twill be larger than the telescope.

EGON
Nary would say the trip merely wasted.
The mathematics and metaphysics
Are favorable for the capture of dead
And imprisoning their unruly souls
To the last syllable of recorded time.

RAY
Wondrous well!
For if the substance whereof all shadows are made be the like,
then achieve we three the cracking of skulls…
In essence spiritual mind you.

PETER
Good Spengler, be you serious this catching of ghosts?

EGON
Aye. Still serious.

PETER
Then, friend Egon, do I revoke the words I spake of thee.
This have I thought good to deliver.

He hands EGON a sweet.

Thou hast earned it.

Exeunt.

Cacao plant of the Americas

SCENE 5

Laboratory. LORD CHANCELLOR stands in wait.

RAY
Limitless are the prospects---Chancellor Yeager!

PETER
I trust thou art ushering us to better lodgings on grounds?

CHANCELLOR
Nay! Thou will be ushered from hence this school.
The board is resolved to end thy grant.
You are banished from these grounds post haste.

PETER
Fie upon it! Explain thyself.

CHANCELLOR
'Tis agreeable.
Nary will this University fund ye studies.

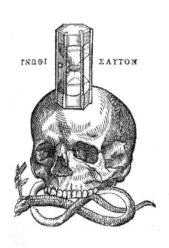

PETER
But loved are we by the youth!

CHANCELLOR
Dr Venkman, believe we the purpose of philosophy be to
serve mankind.
Thou, however, regard philosophy as a stratagem.
Such a deal of skimble-skamble stuff are thy theories as puts
me from my faith.
Slobbery are thy methods.
Conclusions most questionable.
You, sirrah, are a poor philosopher.

PETER
I see.

CHANCELLOR
And thou hast no office within our school.

Exit DEAN YEAGER and EGON.

RAY
And all indign and base adversities
Make head against my estimation!
Forget thee Oxford. Forget St Andrews
For not with pole arm ten metres touch us.

PETER
Reputation is an idle and most false imposition, oft got
without merit and lost without deserving.
You have lost no reputation at all unless you repute yourself
such a loser.
For did not Socrates breathe life into his best work whilst a
stonecutter!

RAY
Knowes't the wages of a stonecutter?

PETER
Nay!

RAY
Admired I the University.
Granted us room and board and hefty coin.
O'er the walls of learning you have not roamed.
Know'est not what the world is like, as I.
Held I positions of the public sort.
Verily, expect they proof of thy labor.

PETER
However the reasons, be it fate or good fortune, ye Fates open
their hands; let thy blood and spirit embrace them;
And, to inure thyself to what thou art like to be, cast thy
humble slough and appear fresh. Believe I we were destined
to be exiled from this blasted heath.

RAY
For what purpose say you?

PETER
To embark 'pon a venture of our choosing.

RAY
This spiritual prison that Sir Spengler and I have put to paper
shall require many a purse of coin.
Wherefore shall we obtain such gold?

PETER
I know not. [*He takes a dram*]
I know not.
                    Exeunt.

MINISTERS OF GRACE
ACT II

ACT 2

SCENE 1

Outside Moneylenders. Enter PETER, RAY, EGON. Fanfare.

PETER
Thou shall regret this not, good cuz.

RAY
Left me by my parents that cottage was.
'twas my inheritance and place of birth!

PETER
Thou shalt not lose thy cottage.
'Tis very common to thrice pawn one's estate.

RAY
But bargain with the moneylender you did not!
Neither a borrower nor a lender be
For loan oft loses both itself and friend

Death and a Moneylender

EGON
For thy knowledge Ray, in sixty months time
Expressed in the condition, an interest
Of seventy thousand ducats wilt thou owe.
Surely a pound of flesh 'twould be a fate less cruel.

PETER
Calm thy nerves. 'Pon the threshold are we three of laying
claim to the foremost spiritual defense philosophy of the next
ten years; Learned spiritual inquisition and banishment.
Rich we shall be beyond our wildest fancy. The world shall be
our oyster, which we with sword will open.

Exeunt.

SCENE 2
Old barn. Enter LANDHOLDER with PETER and EGON.

REAL ESTATE WOMAN
There be offices, sleeping chambers and dining parlour above,
with wine cellar below.

PETER
It seems to me too rich for such a place
That needs repair the violent harms of time.
What think thee, Egon?

EGON
Let the frame of things disjoint then set ablaze.
For her limbs are weak, and her well dried up.
No jutty, frieze, buttress, nor coign of vantage, but this bird
Hath made his pendant bed and procreant cradle.
Whilst in the streets a plague of thieves doth dwell.

RAY
Hark! Be there golden hay on yonder ground?

He jumps down.

Egads! O excellent! When shall we three take up residence?
Try thou must this loft of hay. My belongings shall I bring.
Make our bed here this night.

PETER
I will go and purse the ducats straight.

LANDHOLDER
Wondrous well!
                              Exeunt.

SCENE 3
Ivo Shandor Boarding House.
Enter LADY DANA BARRETT and LOUIS TULLY, a fool.

DANA
God save thee, Master Tully.

LOUIS
Oh, Dana, it is thou!

DANA
Yes, Louis, it is I.

LOUIS
Methought 'twas the apothecary.

DANA
Art thou ill?

LOUIS
Nay, nay, fine my lady. And the fine is, for the which I may go
the finer.

DANA
How hast thou lost thy breath?

LOUIS
By running fast. 'Tis a very excellent piece of work, my lady.
Will it please you to enter in? Some water may I bring thee.

DANA
My thanks to thine offer, but my haste is very great.

LOUIS
I hear no harm. We shall devise the fittest time and safest way.
Many a cask of water have I, the finest in all of London. From
glassy streams of Denmark have it sent.
But this be not news to thine ears.

DANA
Aye, do I know this.

LOUIS
I am just remembered — a revel will I hold in ceremony of four
years on as clerk. And whilst thy cast thine own accompts,
which verily be not wise, I bid thee attend, as I am an honest
neighbor---

DANA
Grant you mercy, Louis, I shall try.

LOUIS
I am just reminded — you should not leave thy wheel a
spinning whilst away. That yonder knave did make complaint
to that our landlord.

DANA
'Tis strange, how could my wheel but spin itself?

LOUIS
Nary concern my lady. For I did spin my wheel with a fury
like that of Mars' chariot, so that all who heard 'twould think
that folly lay in wheels and not their owners.

DANA
Adieu .

LOUIS
Well enow, I shall vouchsafe thee a letter. A gentle bath must I
now conduct —

He attempts to open door, but has locked himself out.
Exit LOUIS.
DANA goes through her mail and picks up a piece of parchment.
Enter PETER, RAY, and EGON to recite the letter.

A spinning wheel.

RAY
Art thou troubled by noises most strange pon' the witching
hour of night?

EGON
Feel thee the pangs of dread in thy cellarage or attic?

PETER
Hast thou or thy kin born witness to demon, apparition, or
ghost?

RAY
If Yay your answer be, make haste and call upon us.

PETER, RAY, EGON
Ministers of Grace!

RAY
Our courteous servants whose sore task does not divide the
Sunday from the week, Be at the ready to defend thee against
the spirits of the dead.

PETER, RAY, EGON
Prepared are we to believe thee!

*DANA tosses the parchment aside and enters kitchen. Lays groceries
out on a table. The eggs begin to tremble, leap out of their shells and
cook on counter. Growling noise from within pantry. DANA opens
pantry door. The spirit world appears in front of her. There is a roar.*

ZUUL
Zuul!

Exeunt.

SCENE 4

Outside The Minister's GARRISON.
PETER stands on a ladder hanging a sign.
JANINE MELNITZ sits at her desk.
Enter RAY pulling a carriage

RAY
Gentle lords, gentle. I have found our carriage.
Needs it new footboard, wheels, axel tree, skeleton boot, rear
quarter…

PETER
The price, pray tell?

RAY
Perchance forty-eight hundred crowns. And mayhap new
spokes, hubs, ….

Exit RAY.

PETER
Janine! Hast thou admitted any messengers?

JANINE
Nay

PETER
Any customers of late?

JANINE
Nay, Doctor Venkman.

PETER
'Tis labour most rewarded. Wilt thy write? Pay we for thine
ink and quill.
Look upon me not. Thou hast the eyes of a water-fly.
Janine! I cry you mercy for my jest of water-flies.
I shall in my office be.

Exit PETER. Enter EGON from beneath JANINE's desk.

JANINE
Thou art very skilled. I can tell what I can tell. Methinks you
keep the company of books.

EGON
Print be dead.

JANINE
Never schooled was I, yet learned.
And some proclaim I be too wise.
Methinks the reading of books be a fine way to pass away the
time. Enjoy I also the sport of tennis, when not to this desk am
chained.
How dost thou pass the time my Lord?

EGON
Collect I cankers, banes, and afflictions.

Exit EGON. Enter DANA.

DANA
Hello? Thy pardon. Be this the place where Ministers of Grace
do dwell?

JANINE
The very same.
What's your will?

DANA
Have I no appointment but wish to plainly speak with one
who will not call me mad.

Enter PETER in a flourish.

I be Peter Venkman. May I be of help?

DANA
I know not. For my story may sound most strange.

PETER
'Tis all we receive the day long. Sit thee down Madam--

DANA
Barrett, Dana Barrett.

PETER
By my troth, you are very well met.

Enter RAY and EGON. They sit and perform tests.

DANA
And heard I a voice cry "Zuul" from within

Stayed I not, but took to my heels post haste
And ne'er have I returned some two days hence.

PETER
'Tis strange such behavior from a pantry.
Think ye the reason be?

DANA
If knew I the cause of the affliction would I not be here.

PETER
What think you Egon? Speak scholarly and wisely.

EGON
I'faith, she does not jest.

DANA
Sooth, I tell you no falsehood. For who would devise a tale as
this?

PETER
Some be those who crave attention.
Whilst others be knaves of the street.

RAY
Mayhap it is a past life intruding pon' the present.

EGON
Long forgotten memories hidden beneath the veil of time.
Nary would I dismiss the gift of sight.

DANA
Your pardon, believe I not such things as these.

PETER
'Tis very well, for neither I.

Yet there be proceedings which we favor
May bring about conclusions to thy cause.

RAY
From the hall of records shall I survey
The plot of situation and the model.
Perchance the building hath a violent past.

PETER
Aye, get thee to that.

EGON
To the literature I shall attend,
In search of demons withal the name of Zuul.

RAY
Pseudomonarchia Daemonum

EGON
Agrippa's Three Books of Occult Philosophy.

RAY
Verily.

PETER
'Tis very well.
And I shall escort the Lady Barrett to her lodgings and look
her 'ore.
Rather, I shall look to her lodgings.

DANA
My thanks to thee kind yet strange sirs.

Exeunt.

SCENE 5

The home of LADY DANA BARRET.
Enter PETER and DANA.

PETER
Whatsoever may befall us, let death take my breath from me
and me alone.

DANA
'Tis the closet.

> PETER *walks to the harpsichord. Plays the two highest notes.*

PETER
They do abhor this. 'Tis torture and not mercy.
> *To the Spirits*
Ho you fiends, you idle creatures you! 'Tis Doctor Venkman!
> *To Dana*
Methinks you could not be bounded in a nutshell and count
thyself a queen of infinite space.
Keep alone?

DANA
Verily

PETER
That is pleasing to my ears.

> *He removes a bellows.*

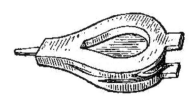

DANA
What mean you sir?

PETER
'Tis scholarly. That for a toy, a thing of no regard.
DANA
That be the bed chamber, but nothing happ'd within.

PETER
'Tis against the rule of nature.

DANA
You be not like the philosopher.

PETER
They be stiff alike in countenance, not in breeding.

DANA
Thou art more a tedious fool.

PETER
Here stands the kitchen?
Mistress Barrett, be these the hatched eggs?

DANA
The very same. For as I stood yonder, lept they from their
shells, and began to cook upon the table.

PETER
'Tis strange indeed.

DANA
And 'twas then I heard such noise from my pantry.
Doctor Venkman, thou hast travelled all this way. I would
you would examine the pantry.

PETER
I shall do so. 'Tis sound advice.

He opens the pantry door.

Zounds!
Behold these vile scraps!

DANA
God's Bread! Nay, this was not here.

PETER
Better this offal thrown into the Thames than touch thy sweet
lips.

DANA
Look ye! This was not here but a void. And in the void a
temple, as if to worship Hades of the Underworld. And all
round the temple flames withal growling beasts, like demon
cur. The flames did rise and on the air did a voice sound Zuul.
Twas' all here, I say!

PETER
I cry your mercy, for there be no proof.

DANA
Well, art thou sure you use your tool correctly?

PETER
By my life, there be no beast within, if by beast you mean this
stake.

DANA
Wondrous well. Be there a monster in my pantry or this may
be some error, and madness hath overtaken me. Ere I eat my
meals in fear, and sleep in the affliction of these terrible

dreams. Better be with the dead, than on the torture of the
mind to lie in restless ecstasy.

PETER
I think thee not mad.

DANA
It calms my nerves to know this.

PETER
Allow me to indulge pon myself. Arrive I home after a day of
labor, and all withal the labor. Be there not a thing in all my
world but work.

DANA
Doctor Venkman --

PETER
I meet your ladyship and by the gods, a like problem has she!

DANA
Verily. The like is thou!

PETER
I shall hazard all. In mine eye thou art the sweetest lady that
ever I looked on.

DANA
Will you hoist sail, sir? Here lies your way.

PETER
And then she bid me pack and out the door
She thought me a knave, she thought me a fool,
And nary was she the first to think such things.

DANA
Thou are art very odd.

PETER
Marry, now I can tell!

DANA
Narry, sir, do not.

PETER
Beloved of me, and that my deeds shall prove!

DANA
'Tis not necessary.

PETER
I shall help thee presently.

DANA
Be content...

PETER
And thou wilt profess that "Peter Venkman be a man of accomplished things!"

DANA
Aye.

PETER
I desire better acquaintance with he.

DANA
Hmm.

PETER
"I do wonder if he so desires better acquaintance?"

DANA
I do wonder.

PETER
Farewell, fair cruelty. Thou wilt think on me after I have gone.

DANA
My Lord I will not.
PETER
What? Deny me of a kiss?

She pushes his face out the door and slams it shut

DANA
Mayhap these spirits that do torment wish me to hell
To stand condemned for pride and scorn.
Then shall I go, but to the gate, and there will the devil meet
me like an
Old cuckold with horns on his head, and say, "Get you to
Heaven, Dana, get you to heaven; here's no place for you
Maids."
So deliver I up my apes and away to Saint Peter.
For the heavens, he shows me where the bachelors sit, and
there
Live we as merry as the day is long.
Yet if Saint Peter this be he, then contempt, farewell, and
maiden pride, adieu!
No glory lives behind the back of such.

Exit DANA.

MINISTERS OF GRACE
ACT III

ACT 3

SCENE 1
Music. Enter PETER, RAY, and EGON above.
They sit and dine.

PETER
Let us drink to our premier patron.

RAY
To our first and only patron.

PETER
I have need of pocket coin. To sup with Lady Barrett 'twould
be wise. We do not wish to lose her.

RAY
This magnificent feast you see before thee represents the last
of our coffers.

PETER
Peace. Chew thy food.

Enter JANINE. She sits at desk. Enter MESSENGER.

MESSENGER
If Ministers of Grace this be the home
And if they be not altogether fool
Then the message I bear I bear for thee.
From Peddler's Inn have I herto implore thine aid this night.
A grim grinning ghost have we, that torments
Weary travelers, and chases them away
But discretion be the key, for not all
Who stay at Peddler's Inn have borne witness.

JANINE
I will charm them first to keep their tongue
Then I shall sound the bell that we have one!

She rings a bell.

RAY
An alarum! Make haste!

They exit (jumping from hay loft)
They Re-enter below, dress in haste, and board the ECTO carriage.
A black cat yowls like a siren. EGON rings a bell.

Exeunt.

Ringing bells.

SCENE 2

An Inn. Enter PETER, RAY, EGON in a flourish.

PETER
Hath any here seen a ghost?

A pretty maid walks past. They all stare appreciatively.
Enter INNKEEPER.

INNKEEPER
I humbly thank thee gentles for thy speed.
Our guests grow anxious by the hour and start
To question me for reasons have I none.

RAY
Hath it appeared ere now?

INNKEEPER
The eldest servants know of higher floor
The strange impatience, I do mean to say
Though stirred it not these past five moons till late.
And ne're did carry on as violently.

EGON
Did'st thou make report to any soul?

INNKEEPER
Nay! Good heavens! We do not speak of it.
I wish it were removed before the dawn.

RAY
Verily. Now peace good sir. Custom hath made it in we a
property of easiness.

Exit INNKEEPER

MAN AT STAIRS
What be you, a Muscovite?

PETER
Nay, we be extirpators. A rat a man did see on floors above
and called upon us.

MAN
An unholy size this rat must be.

PETER
'Twould take this from this, sirrah.

RAY
Wilt thou follow?

An inn.

MAN
I'd rather keep my head to chew and swallow.

RAY
It hath occurred to me of late that a successful trial of our
weapons have we not.

EGON
I do accuse myself.

PETER
As do I.

RAY
The fault, dear Egon, is not in our stars but in ourselves, that
we are underlings.

PETER
Wherefore be troubled?
For upon our backs have we unlicensed boxes of rough magic.

RAY
Agreed. Are we content ?

EGON charges RAY's pack, then stands apace.
Enter a CHAMBERMAID.
RAY and EGON shout and blast her cart with beams of light.

PETER
Hold!

CHAMBERMAID
What, i' th' name of God?

EGON
I cry your pardon.

PETER
Pardon

RAY
I beg thee mercy.

PETER
Methoght you were another.
[beat]
Successful trial?

RAY
Verily. Divide our group in three to hunt this apparition?

PETER
Aye, for greater damage may we accomplish.

> *Exit PETER and EGON. RAY lights his pipe.*
> *ENTER SLIMER, a ghost.*

RAY
Hark! Venkman!
Detested cloakbag of guts!
Needs must I hold it here.

> *He fires at the spirit. Exit SLIMER and RAY.*
> *Enter PETER*

Sees SLIMER. Calls to offstage

PETER
Hark, Ray.

RAY
Saw it with mine eyes!
And then it started like a guilty thing
Upon a fearful summons.

PETER
It be here, Ray. And pierces me with it's gaze.

RAY
There is not ugly a fiend of hell as he shalt be.
Is it not so?

PETER
Methinks it hears the words you speak, good Ray.

RAY
Hold! 'twill not harm thee.

SLIMER flies at PETER. Enter RAY

Good sir Peter! Art thou well? Speak! What horrors hath yond
illusion dealt thee?

PETER
I have had a most rare vision
Where it hath oozed pon me a foul slime.

RAY
Wondrous well! Can thou move?

EGON

Offstage

If thou canst hear my words, then answer them.

PETER
Man's hand is not able to taste, his tongue to conceive, nor his heart to report what I do feel.

RAY
Good sir Spengler! I am presently with Venkman. Oozed o'r with slime is he!

EGON
Excellent well! Retrieve thee a cup. Now prithee, come hither. The ghost hath entered the banquet. The game's a foot!

Exeunt.

SCENE 3

A Ballroom. Enter SLIMER.

SLIMER
In life I was Sir John Belushi called;
And burned the nightly candle keeping wassail.
Till that fateful hour upon the solemn feast
With eager feeding food did choke the feeder.
Now doom'd for a certain term to walk the night,
Sans legs, sans feet, sans taste, sans everything.
And for the day confined to fast in fires,
Till the foul crimes done in my days of nature
Are burnt and purged away.
What then? Shall there be no more cakes and ale?
Must I be bound and laid in some dark room
As these three rogues intend for me? But nay!
An honest man am I, and hates the slime
That sticks on filthy deeds.

Slimer. Illustration by Jordan Monsell

ENTER The Ministers behind a curtain.
RAY scans with his ecto-spectacles.
SLIMER floats to chandelier.

RAY
Look where it comes again upon the vault.

PETER
Tis the very same that slimed me o're.

EGON
He is as disproportioned in his manners as in his shape.

RAY
At the ready? Now!

They fire. The chandelier falls.

RAY
'Tis no fault but my own!

PETER
All's well. The table did break its fall.

EGON
There be something of moment I neglected to impart.

PETER
What, mind you?

EGON
Ne're cross ye streams.

PETER
Wherefore?

EGON
'Twould be ill favored.

PETER
I be not clear twixt good and bad. What mean you ill favored?

EGON
Imagine if you will thy life taken
Instantly in corporal sufferance and
Each fiber of thyself blown with restless
Violence roundabout the pendent world.

RAY
Tis a vile thing to die when men are unprepared and look not
for it.

PETER
That is bad. A most important proclamation of health and
safety. Do not cross ye streams. My humble thanks Egon.
Tis very well. Prithee Ray, vouchsafe me aid upon the left.
Egon, pon the right.

RAY fires.

Egon!

EGON fires.

Hold! Hold! Cease! O, happy shooting mousquetaire!

RAY
He is weary, but will move again! Prithee, turn the tables up
and give me space enough to lay the trap.

PETER
Wait, hold. I great desire I have for this.

He pulls a tablecloth knocking everything o're but a vase.

And the flowers that which here stands up!

RAY places a trap.

RAY
Await my signal. Spengler, confine him in a stream. Go! The trap is lain!

EGON fires.

Good enow, hold him lest he move. Go!

PETER fires.

EGON
A hit! A palpable hit!

RAY
Needs must you bring him down whilst not crossing thy streams.

PETER
Mayhap now you wilt nary gentleman slime withal a magic musket?

EGON
Venkman, prithee shorten thy stream! I wish not my visage burned to cinder!

RAY
Very well. I shall ope the trap. Look not at it's harsh light!

He opens the trap.

EGON
I gazed upon the trap, Ray.

RAY
Bring ye streams off whilst I close the trap. Prepare thee.
Closing---now!

RAY closes the trap. PETER and EGON cease firing.

Be contented. Anon!

EGON
It is within.

PETER
Oy!

RAY
Ah, sirrah, this unlooked-for sport comes well.

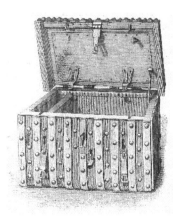

Enter INNKEEPER.

PETER
Venimus, vidimus, nos non asinum calce!

INNKEEPER
Did'st thou bear witness? Pray, what manner of creature be it?

RAY
We hath captured the spirit!

INNKEEPER
What be it? Wilt there be more?

RAY
Touching this vision here,
It is an honest ghost, that let me tell you.
What we name a phantom repeating and focused in nature;
Vaporous and full roaming within the class of five.

PETER
Now, let us speak plain and to the purpose.
For the capture, a fee of four thousand crown we needs must ask.
Yet seeing as the beast must be inured, a fee of one thousand crowns be it your pleasure.

INNKEEPER
Five thousand crowns? I did not think 'twould cost as much. I won't pay.

PETER
Tis very well!
Release the ghost at once therein
To haunt again this very inn.

RAY
Verily Doctor Venkman.

INNKEEPER
Nay! I am content, in faith. I'll seal to such a bond!

PETER
We humbly thank you, sir.

RAY
Our thanks to thee! Make clear the path!
Full roaming apparition. Look to thyselves!

Exeunt.

SCENE 4

The streets of London. Enter four town criers (CHORUS). As they give the news, the Ministers of Grace and townsfolk scurry past.

ROGER GRIMSBY
Hear ye, Hear ye, I be Roger Grimsby
The whole of England alive with prattle
Of stories strange and rank in nature.
Visions of dead men, their chains a rattle
From London to the English Channel.

JOE FRANKLIN
Round the fire's glow hath we all been told
Of ghostly tales to freeze thy blood
Ev'n my grandmother would a tale unfold
Of spectral chariots through fields of mud

LARRY KING
I be Larry of the King
And wish to speak of ghostly things
These exorcists whom some praise sing
Whilst others blame for everything.

CASEY KASEM
These Ministers of Grace defend us still
At the playhouse Rose did they nobly guard
The knights of gray smote the dead with skill
And remained to dance the galliard.

Enter PETER

PETER
From the break of day to the last crowing of the cock.
Nary a task too large!
Nary a fee to large!

Exeunt.

Galliard

SCENE 5

Ministers of Grace GARRISON. Enter JANINE. She sits at desk.
Enter WINSTON. He sits.

JANINE
Believe the following superstitions;
Hobgoblins, sprites, and fairies of the wood
Witches, their sorcery, and beasts from hell
Banshees and harpies that do no one good
And Atlantis lost to the ocean swell?

WINSTON
If there be a hefty pound of gold therein
Then take suggestion as a cat laps milk.

Enter PETER and RAY, carrying traps.

RAY
O weary night, O long and tedious night, needs must I sleep.

PETER
You look not well.

RAY
Be it so?

PETER
Looked you better favored in prior days.
These be the papers from St. Albans. Paid she on credit.

JANINE
And be these the tasks for this evening.

RAY
Twice more unto the breach.

JANINE
This be Winston, the Moor of Zedda
Come to inquire in the office of Minister.

RAY
Of good news! The office is thine.
I be Ray Stantz, this Pete Venkman.
Well go thy ways. Prithee, may you stead me?

He hands WINSTON the traps.

Exeunt.

MINISTERS OF GRACE

ACT IV

ACT 4

SCENE 1

Music Hall. Enter PETER, DANA and VIOLINIST severally.

DANA
Wilt thou attend on me a moment?

VIOLINIST
I shall my lady.

She goes to PETER

DANA
Doctor Venkman, I stand surprisèd.

PETER
'Twas a rehearsal most lovely.

DANA
O, thou heard?

PETER
In all your row, thou art the best.

DANA
My humble thanks. You have a skilled ear in music, for most
cannot hear me play 'amongst the rest.

PETER
I have no need of thy abuse and scorn
Have I throngs that lay in wait to do so.

DANA
Verily. Renownèd cross the land art thou.
Gather so much as from occasion you may glean,
Whether aught, to me unknown, afflicts my domicile?

PETER
What's he that stands rigid like a dead man?

DANA
The dead man plays most fine o' the viol-de-gamboys.
Now I pray thee speak in sober judgment.

PETER
Verily, but wish I vouchsafe you this in private.

DANA
For what reason I beseech you?

PETER
Ay, marry.
The name of Zuul have I found in our books.
A demi-god praised some six thousand years Before our Lord
by the...what be this word?

DANA
Hittites.

PETER
Hittites, the Mesopotamians and the Sumerians.

DANA
Zuul 'twas the minion of Gozer. What be this Gozer?

PETER
Renowned was he in Sumeria.

DANA
Wherefore does he idle in my pantry so?

PETER
In faith, I have set upon the task. Perchance thou would sup
with me on Thursday next, when the cock crows nine, and an
exchange of knowledge we shall undertake.

DANA
Thou art the bluntest wooer in all Christendom.
I cannot see thee Thursday next, for I am busy!

PETER
Mistress Barrett, seem you to think there be a malady of the
mind that speaks:
He delights some little time so by his companies.

Hittites

But nay, forsooth, I take pains in thy case.
For you in my respect as an artist be.
And as a lady of high fashion, for you do put on your best
attire this day.

DANA
Anon. I shall thee Thursday.

VIOLINIST
What's he?

DANA
A friend.

VIOLINIST
A friend?

DANA
Verily. An old friend.

PETER
                              [Calling]
I shall see thee anon! Thy pardon — I did not meet thee, sirrah!
A good health to you. Thou art still marvelous pale about the
face however! Mayhap some sun…

VIOLINIST
What does he?

DANA
He be a philosopher.

VIOLINIST
I marvel your ladyship takes delight in such a barren rascal.
Look you now, he's out of his guard already. Unless you

laugh and minister occasion to him, he is gagged.

DANA
Oh, you are sick of self-love, and taste with a distempered
appetite.

Exit all but PETER.

PETER
Would the night were come!
By this day she's a fair lady.
I do spy some marks of love in her.
If it proves so, then loving goes by haps;
Some Cupid kills with arrows, some with traps.

PETER *spins about as music plays.*
He Exits.

SCENE 2

Ministers of Grace GARRISON. Enter RAY and WINSTON.

RAY
This be where we imprison all the spirits, demons, and those
that would slime.
Since brevity is the soul of wit, and tediousness the limbs and
outward flourishes, I will be brief.
When Saint Elmo's Fire is seen, the trap will be clean. The
apparition is interred within our holy sepulcher.

Enter PETER and JANINE.

JANINE
There is at the gate a gentleman from the Ministry of Lands
much desires to speak with you.

PETER
What does he wish?

JANINE
I know not but this; a fortnight have I labored here with nary a
respite.
Thou warrant me assistance in this task.

PETER
Janine, one withal thy skills would no trouble finding
employment as a tavern wench or midwife.

JANINE
Better masters have I quit.

Enter MESSENGER.

Ministers! What is your will?!

Exit all but PETER. Enter WALTER PECK

PETER
May I help thee?

PECK
My name is Walter Peck. Of the Ministry of Protected Lands,
His Grace's third region.

PETER
We are well met.
He slaps PECK on the back with slime.
How goes it there?

PECK
Art thou Peter Venkman called?

PETER
Verily, I am Doctor Venkman.

PECK
And of what degree of physic art thou, Master Venkman?

PETER
Achieved I have degrees in philosophy and alchemy.

PECK
I see. And now thou catch ghosts?

PETER
If one wished to say it so.

PECK
And how many ghosts have thou caught, Master Venkman?

PETER
I cannot say.

PECK
And wherefore dost thou imprison these ghosts upon
capture?

PETER
Confined they to a holy sepulcher.

Alchemists at work.

PECK
And 'twould this tomb upon these grounds be kept?

PETER
Verily

PECK
And may I see withal mine eye this sepulcher?

PETER
Nay

PECK
By what rule, Master Venkman?

PETER
For thou did not speak the word most magical.

PECK
And what be the word most magical, Master Venkman?

PETER
Please!

PECK
Mary, may I please see withal mine eye the holy sepulcher?

PETER
Wherefore wish you to see our prison cell?

PECK
But for a satisfaction of my thought.
I would wot more of what thou do here.
The people cry out fanciful stories,
And wish we to determine the impact
Thy operation has pon' the King's land.

Exempli gratia, the presence of foul and filthy air in thy
cellarage! Now either thou reveal'st to me what lay
Beneath the boards that we doth stand upon
Or return I with documents of court.

PETER
Get thee gone and retrieve your documents.
I shall see thee for the judge in false report.

PECK
Thou can have it thy way, Master Venkman.

Exit PETER.

PECK
I am determined to prove a villain
And hate the idle pleasures of these days.
Plots shall I lay, inductions dangerous,
To set the Lord Mayor and these mountebanks
In deadly hate, the one against the other;
And if Lord Mayor be as true and just
As I am subtle, false, and treacherous,
Then soon shall each a halter 'bout the neck
And all will know my name is Walter Peck

Exit PECK. Enter RAY, EGON, and WINSTON

EGON
I fear, good Ray, the thronging spirits that we hold grows to
so great a bulk.
I can withal mine eye, within the compass of the horizon,
As 'twere a rising bubble in the sea, a thing most great and
terrible in nature.

WINSTON
What mean you great?

EGON
Let us say this tart* be the standard amount of spiritual
fortitude withal London.
Given the sample taken this morn, 'twould be a tart five and
thirty feet in length
with a weight thirty score pounds.

WINSTON
That be a great tart.

Enter PETER.

PETER
A visit have we had of late from Ministry of Protected Lands.
How doth our tomb?

RAY
Nary well.

WINSTON
Reveal to him of the tart

PETER
What of the tart?

Exeunt.

SCENE 3
The rooftop of the Ivo Shandor Building. Thunder. Lightning.
A stone gargoyle comes to life.

VOICE OF GOZER
'Tis time; descend; be stone no more; approach;
Strike all that look upon with marvel. Come,
I'll fill your grave up: stir, nay, come away.

SCENE 4
Ivo Shandor Boarding House. Thunder and Lightning.
Enter DANA. LOUIS runs out to greet her.
Music is heard within

LOUIS
Oh, Dana, it's thou!

DANA
Greetings Louis.

LOUIS
Needs must you enter in!
Of merriness you have lost the sight of.

DANA
Would I were free Master Louis, but alas, I am engaged.

LOUIS
Thou art engaged this very night?

DANA
Thy pardon Louis, into a thousand that I have forgotten.

LOUIS
All be well. Thou may herald him hence.

DANA
Perchance we two will make acquaintance.

LOUIS
Good as the best!
I shall announce thine arrival post haste. Play we a game of
barley-break and dance a jib.
Gentles all —
Ho, open the door! I pray thee, let me in!

*Exit LOUIS. DANA enters room. There is a knock
Enter MESSENGER.*

DANA
How now?

MESSENGER
I humbly do entreat your ladyship's pardon;
Your mother most desires to speak with you.

DANA
I bid thee, go you and tell her I am engaged.

MESSENGER
To be wed?

DANA
Thou art a wise fool.
Marriage may his purpose be.

MESSENGER
What may I tell her be his office?

DANA
Tell her a Minister of Grace be he.

MESSNGER
They that —

DANA
Aye. That the Caps, hands, and tongues of the rabble applaud
to the clouds.
Here's for thy pains. Go and bid her good health and father's
too. I shall call on her anon.

Exit MESSENGER

Sound of growling

*Arms reach from the chair to grab her. The Door opens.
A terror dog within.*

DANA
Avaunt, and quit my sight! Let the earth hide thee.
My bones are marrowless, my blood is cold.
Thou hast no speculation in those eyes
Which thou dost glare with!

Exit DANA dragged through door.

SCENE 5
The home of LOUIS TULLY. Music. Guests mingle.

TALL MAIDEN
Louis, I take my leave of thee.

LOUIS
Nay, good lady. Mayhap if we cut a caper, the rest will fall in.

TALL MAIDEN
Very well.

Knock at door

LOUIS
I bid thee welcome Theodore and Annette
From township Fleming if I'm not mistake
A merchant Theodore be of Persian rugs
And makes a handsome purse of coin might add.

Now which of you doth wish to play at dice?

Growling.

And who did bring the dog against advice?

*ENTER Terror dog. Party guests scream.
Exit LOUIS pursued by dog.*

ENTER LOUIS and dog.

LOUIS
O monsterou! Sackerson is let loose! Give me some help! – O,
cruel!
I shall complaint at Tenant's parley next.
Let me enter! I cry your mercy let me enter!

Sweet hound, sweet and gentle hound. Perchance a table scrap
have I....

Darkness.

SCENE 6

Outside Ivo Shandor Boarding House.
Enter DOORMAN, GUARD, and PETER severally

PETER
What has befall'n here?

GUARD
'Twas a fool that brought a bear to revelry and let loose it did
with mortal rage.

PETER
I am here to see the Lady Barrett.

> *DOORMAN shows him in*

> *PETER knocks on DANA's door.*

PETER
Greetings.

> *DANA has become ZUUL.*

This be a new habit for thee, is it not?

DANA
Art thou the Master of Keys?

PETER
I be not aware of such title given'.

> *She slams the door. He knocks again.*

DANA
Be thou the Master of Keys?

PETER
Aye!
I be a friend of his. He bid me meet him here. Thy name,
however, escapes me.

DANA
I am Zuul called. The Porter of the Gate.

PETER
Wherefore thy actions be this day, Zuul?

DANA
Prepare we must, for the coming of Gozer.

PETER
And who be this Gozer thou speak of now?

DANA
The Destructor.

PETER
Are we still to dine together? 'Tis customary to clean your
domicile when guests thou art expecting.

DANA
Wish you this flesh?

PETER
                    [aside]
But 'tis strange.
And oftentimes, to win us to our harm,
The instruments of darkness tell us truths,
Win us with honest trifles, to betray 's
In deepest consequence.

                To DANA

Thou are a Sphinx and this be a riddle?
'Twould appear the roses can cast a spell.

DANA
Take me now, unbefitting creature.

PETER
Converse we so little.

                She grabs him.

DANA
Wish I were you inside me.

PETER
Why then, let fall your horrible pleasure!
Nay, I mustn't. For it seems that two persons inhabit thee
And three 'twould cause a bulk.
Forgo thine attempts to disturb me thus
And lay thy head against this pillow here.
Wish I to speak with Dana. Tis Peter.
Wish I to speak with Lady Dana now.

DANA
There be no Dana. Be only Zuul.

PETER
Zuulie, you jest. I do beseech you, wish I to speak with Dana.
Lady Dana.
Calm thyself and henceforth bring Dana hither.

The voice of ZUUL emanates her.

DANA
There be no Dana. Be only Zuul!

PETER
Thy song like the nightingale must be.
Now hear me demon I shall count to three,
If Dana hear I not will trouble be.
One! Two!...
DANA's eyes flutter and turn white
Two and a half!

The voice of ZUUL screams. DANA rises above the bed.

Prithee descend.

ZUUL roars. Darkness.

Levitation

SCENE 7

Kensington Gardens. Enter LOUIS.
He has become Vinz Clortho. He runs madly about.

LOUIS
I be the Master of Keys! The Destructor will approach! The
Traveler! The Destroyer! Porter of the Gate!

Enter a Horse and Wagon. LOUIS addresses the horse.

Be I Vinz Clortho called, the Master of Keys to Gozer,
Volguus Zildrohar, Lord of all Sebouillia.
Art thou the Porter of the Gate?

COACHMAN
Pulls he the wagon, but make I the sales. Wish thou a ride?

LOUIS growls.

LOUIS
                    [to the horse]
What fools these mortals be!
Attend the sign, and our prisoners shall be released.
He Exits, yelling.
Thou shalt perish in flame!
Attend the sign! Anon the Porter of the Gate I find!

COACHMAN
What an ass!

Exeunt.

SCENE 8

Outside Ministers of Grace GARRISON. Enter GUARDS with
LOUIS in shackles. GUARD knocks. Enter JANINE

JANINE
Dost thou deliver or take from hence?

GUARD
I do deliver madam.

JANINE
But a moment.

Enter EGON.

GUARD
Art thou a Minister of Grace?

EGON
Aye, in sooth.

GUARD
Found we this loon
As mad as the vexed sea, singing aloud,
Crowned with rank fumiter and furrow-weeds.
Afeard we are to hold him in the Tower
Thus at your gates and humbly ask your will.
To draw him on to pleasures, and to gather,
So much as from occasion you may glean,
Whether aught, to us unknown, afflicts him thus,
That, open'd, lies within your remedy.

LOUIS
Art thou the Porter of the Gate?

EGON
Methinks it best if you usher him in.

JANINE
Charitable thou art towards such dredges of humanity
To commit this man unto thy care.

EGON
Believe I not he human.

Exit GUARDS.

EGON
What say your name be?

LOUIS
Vinz Clortho, the Master of Keys to Lord Gozer.

JANINE
According to his papers, he is Louis Tully called.
From yonder Smithfield does he reside.
Wish you a pot of ale Master Tully?

LOUIS
Wish I?

EGON
Aye, partake.

LOUIS
Aye, partake.

EGON
Spoke thee of awaiting a sign. Prithee, what be this sign?

LOUIS
Gozer the Traveler! Come will he in one of the pre-chosen
forms. Whilst during the Rectification of the Vuldronaii, the
Traveler came he as a large and moving Torb! Then, whilst
during the Third Reconciliation of the Last of the Meketrex
Supplicants, chose they a new form for he, that of a giant
Sloar! Many Shubs and Zuuls knew what it t'was to be roasted
in the depths of a Sloar that day, I can tell thee!

JANINE
Egon?

EGON
Thy pardon.

JANINE
There be something marvelous strange about that man.
Faith, a soothsayer might I be, for some certain dregs of
conscience are yet within me.
I am afeard death will befall you.

They embrace. A MESSENGER enters. LOUIS jumps.

Giant Sloar

EGON
I shall attend to it.

LOUIS *attempts to take the note.*

My thanks. I have it.

Enter PETER composing the letter, and DANA, asleep on a bed.

EGON
Tis from Peter. He brings tidings from the realm of Gozer.

JANINE
What says he?

EGON
He is in the company of Mistress Barrett. 'Twould seem the demon woos his wife to be.

JANINE
How fares she?

PETER
She appears, as I write this, like a beast
Forth at her eyes her spirits wildly peep;
And, as the sleeping soldiers in the alarm,
Her bedded hair, like life in excrements,
Starts up, and stands on end.
Gave her I the seeds of the poppy
So that sleep may cause her some relief.
Says she be the Porter of the Gate
Make sense to thee this name?

EGON composes a letter to PETER.

EGON
Mayhap it does, for met I now the Master of Keys.

He gives letter to the MESSENGER who brings it to PETER.
PETER reads and then responds.

PETER
Wondrous well. We needs must introduce the one to the
other.

Letter is sent back to EGON. EGON writes.

EGON
I believe 'twould be most retrograde to our desire.

MESSENGER takes letter to PETER.
He reads, then writes a response

PETER
Then I bid you hold him, I shall be there anon.

MESSENGER –now short of breath--takes letter back to EGON.
EGON reads the letter. A cock crows.

EGON
I wish we had bestowed that time.

To JANINE

We must seek out Ray. I have need of him presently.

Exit all but PETER and DANA.

PETER
I have some ill-fated news. I must anon.
Whilt thou stay hither in bed until I return?

I take my leave of you. Shall not be long but I'll be here again.

He kisses her and Exits.

MINISTERS OF GRACE
ACT V

ACT 5

SCENE 1

A road outside London. WINSTON drives the Ecto carriage.
RAY is studying a scroll.

WINSTON
Friend Ray, have you faith in the Almighty God?

RAY
I cannot say, as our paths have not crossed.

WINSTON
Verily, do I. And love the Savior's bearing I'faith.

RAY
...this lancet arch is made of stone not found on English soil.

WINSTON
Thou appear vexed, my friend, what have you there?

RAY
They be the model wherein resides the Mistress Barett, and
they are marvelous strange indeed.

WINSTON
Dost thou recall a passage from the Holy Book, when the
graves stood tenantless and the sheeted dead did squeak and
gibber in the streets ?

RAY
I recall Revelation 7:12.
And I looked, as he opened the sixth seal,

And behold, there was a mighty earthquake,
And the sun became as black as sackcloth.
And all the moon became as blood.

WINSTON
And the seas boiled and the skies fell.
And prologue to the omen coming on,
Have heaven and earth together demonstrated
Unto our climatures and countrymen.

RAY
The Day of Judgment.

WINSTON
The Day of Judgment.

"Last Judgment" - Pieter Bruegel the Elder c.1590

RAY
To each his own religion, fables told
As harbingers preceding still the fates
The end of days and such.

WINSTON
Fables, nay. Hath it not occurred to thee
Perchance the reason of such engagement
As of late is for the dead have risen?

RAY
If music be the food of comfort—

WINSTON
Play on.

RAY reveals a flute and begins to play.

Exeunt.

SCENE 2

Inside Ministers of Grace GARRISON. *Enter PECK with*
GUARD CAPTAIN and BLACKSMITH.

PECK
Follow thee.

Enter JANINE.

JANINE
Pardon thee. Thy pardon, gentles. Wherefore go you?

PECK
Stand you awhile aloof or I shall have thee shackled for
impeachment.

JANINE
I would know thy purpose, sirrah. For knowest I the law —
enter not without a warrant.

PECK reads a scroll.

PECK
Forbear all commerce, extent of thy house and lands, ban of
public allowances for unauthorized handlers of waste, and a
Royal order for entry and survey.

Exit PECK, GUARD CAPTAIN, BLACKSMITH, and JANINE.
Enter EGON and LOUIS

EGON
Vinz, a final test I wish to perform on thee —

Enter JANINE with PECK, GUARD and BLACKSMITH behind.

JANINE

He is here at the door, and importunes access. What is to be
said to him? He's fortified against any denial.

EGON
Thy pardon, your feet tread on private ground!

PECK
Cease the instruments and open yonder doors.

EGON
I pray you take care. If break thou this seal, a peril will befall
us this day.

PECK
I'll tell thee what be perilous. Thou face prosecution from the
King for half a dozen crimes 'gainst the land.
Now cease these false instruments or we shall in thy stead.

EGON
Be warned. For this trick may chance to scathe you.
Ope' the ponderous and marble jaws,
Of this holy sepulcher, wherein hath
We inurn'd the souls of countless dead
What mean you this , to cast them up again?
Revisit'st them the glimpses of the moon,
Making night hideous; and we fools of nature
Withal thoughts beyond the reaches of our souls?

PECK
Patronize me not. I be not a dullard as they you cheat!

Enter PETER.

PETER
Peace, good sir for I be Peter Venkman.
'Twould appear a misprised mood infects the' air

And wish I to abet it in any way.

PECK
Begone or talk not, I advise you. Forget thou the shames that
thou hast stained me?
I have too long borne your blunt upbraidings and thy bitter
scoffs. Well now 'tis my turn.

EGON
Desires he to unleash hell upon us.

PETER
Whatsoever my befall us, the blame wilt be on thy head.

PECK
Nay, 'twill be on thine.

PETER
Nay! We shall not be held liable for thy mistakes.

PECK
Break the seal!

PETER
Break any breaking here, and I'll break thy knave's pate.

BLACKSMITH
The likes of this I have ne'er lain eyes on.

PECK
Thine opinion interests me not. Simply break the seal.

PETER stops the BLACKSMITH.

PETER
My friend, be not a fool.

GUARD
Avant!

PECK
If speaketh he again, thou may slay him.

GUARD
Peace, thou ginger painted maypole.
Carry out thy own task, and I shall do the like.

PETER
My thanks to thee, sir.

PECK
Break the seal!

BLACKSMITH
Much danger do I undergo for thee.

> *He pries open the doors. An alarum sounds.*
> *Lights flash. Walls tremble.*

BLACKSMITH
Blast!

EGON
Be gone! Get thee to safety!

> *All Exeunt in haste.*

> *Explosions. Pink streams of spiritual energy emerge.*
> *A Crowd gathers. ENTER LOUIS and JANINE*

LOUIS
This be it! This be the sign!

He Exits.

JANINE
Tis a sign, in faith--of closing shoppe.

Enter RAY, WINSTON, GUARDS, PETER, EGON, PECK, and CONSTABLE'S MEN severally.

RAY
What has befallen here?

EGON
The sepulcher has been opened. He broke the seal.

RAY
O, fie upon it!

WINSTON
This be bad, is it not?

RAY
Aye.

PETER
Where be the Master of Keys?

EGON
Zounds!

RAY
What's he that Master of Keys is called thus?

EGON
Follow thee!

PECK
Hold! I wish these men in chains, being criminals in violation
of the King's Lands.
This blast you see before you be on them!

EGON
Thy mother –

They fight. CONSTABLE'S men try to keep order. Exeunt.

ENTER ghosts in a Dance Macabre. The CROWD runs in fear.
ENTER DANA as the ghosts dance around her in a frenzy.

Exeunt.

Danse Macabre

SCENE 3

A prison cell in the Tower of London.

WINSTON
Whence came this restraint? I would send a letter! Although I
am in their employment, I'd have thee know I was not
present!

EGON
The fabric of the vault be alike in
Telescopes of Galileo Galilei
To gaze upon unnumber'd sparks above.

RAY
Buttresses withal touchstones pure of gold.

PETER
Mark them well my friends? It is a matter of small
consequence. The masons built them not as they once did.

Galileo

RAY
Nay! Ne're did they ever construct them in this fashion. Either the master mason was of the sharpest sort, or a mad fool whose craft be pleasing to the eye!

PETER
Ray, your words are a very fantastical banquet. Just so many strange dishes. Pray tell, in plain English speak, what fray is upon us?

RAY
Thou studied not. Constructed he the building for purpose of beckoning spiritual convocation. Thy ladyship, good Sir Peter, resides in corner penthouse of Apparition Tower.

PETER
She be not my ladyship, good cousin.
A keen interest have I, in sooth, tis true
For we be in her employment as such.
Lay above her bed sheets did I mention?
Yet bed sheet touch not her skin in this sport.
I love to hear her speak yet well I know
That music hath a far more pleasing sound;

EGON
Tis not the Lady Barrett but the house.
Something wicked this way comes, and her home
Clearly be the door through which it enter in.
Chief architect was Ivo Shandor called
Anno domini 1523 did he find
An alliance most secret in nature.

PETER
If I may divine: they who worshipped Gozer.

EGON
Aye.

PETER
Studied not!

EGON
When smoke had cleared from Crusades long had fought
Shandor was resolved that mankind be too sick.
Stand alone in such belief was he not.
A thousand acolytes followed him in death.
As was their custom, met on rooftop high
Custom most horrible,'twould bring about
Doomsday upon the souls of every man.
Now 'twould appear it may befall us all.

PETER
[singing]
So be gentle for Jove's sake
Ho-nonny. Something wicked…

Gozer worshipers

RAY
We needs must leave this place and seek a judge;
A rightful judge. An upright, learned judge.

WINSTON
Hold! Night and silence! Suggest we declare a god of Babylon,
whose influence was mouldy ere our grandsires had nails on
their toes, shall descend pon Blackfriars and destroy our faire
city?

RAY
Sumerian, not Babylonian.

PETER
Aye, much difference!

WINSTON
Thy pardon gentlemen, needs must I send for a lawyer;
Aye, but who comes here?

JAILER
The Lord Mayor requires your haste-post-haste appearance,
Even on the instant. It is a business of some heat as
All the city hath been mired in madness.
Prithee follow, and I shall take you hence.

The Tower of London

PETER
Regretfully I take my leave of thee
As Lord Mayor wishes chatter with me.

Exit JAILER with PETER, RAY, EGON, and WINSTON

SCENE 4
Remnants of DANA's domicile. Enter LOUIS.

LOUIS
I be the Master of Keys!

DANA
The Porter of the Gate be I; Now come,
Insert thy key and caress me hard,
As if you plucked up kisses by the roots
That grow upon my lips, then lay your leg
Over my thigh, and sigh, and kiss, and then
Cry "Cursed we that give ourselves to Gozer!"

They kiss, then ascend the stairs to the Temple of Gozer.

Exeunt.

SCENE 5

Office of the LORD MAYOR.
Enter MAYOR, followed by CONSTABLE, and GUARDS

MAYOR
Before me lay a city wracked with fear
And no advice do my advisers give
Come forth and give us better news, I pray!

CONSTABLE
The troops have barricaded the roads, my Lord.

GUARD
The Ministers of Grace have arrived, my Lord.

MAYOR
The Ministers, yes, The Ministers. I say, where be the man
they call Peck? Let him approach.

Enter PECK, followed by the MINISTERS.

PECK
I Walter Peck am called thy Liege.
Prepared am I to deliver my report.
Guilty these four souls be of cozenage,
As nimble jugglers that deceive the eye,
Dark-working sorcerers that change the mind,
Soul-killing witches that deform the body,
Disguised cheaters, prating mountebanks,
And many suchlike liberties of sin.
There`s no composition in this news that gives them credit.
These knaves you see before you speak falsely.

RAY
All 'twas well till our prison was opened by this eunuch here.

PECK
Caused they the blast, my Lord!

MAYOR
Be this true?

PETER
Aye, tis' true. This man be gelded.

CONSTABLE
Part the fray, part the fray!

PETER
To the selfsame tune and words!

MAYOR
Peace! Thou art at court! Now wherefore shall I do Sir John?
What say'st thou to this?

FIRE COMMISIONER
'Twas no twinkling of stars or northern lights we were
witnessed to this morn.
There were drawn
Upon a heap a hundred ghastly women,
Transformed with their fear, who swore they saw
Men all in fire walk up and down the streets.
Seen, have I, all matter of combustion,
From bird-bolts to canon bullets.
But I am vexed.

CONSTABLE
The walls of Baynard Castle
Like a fountain with an hundred spouts,
Did run pure blood.
How dost thou explain such a curse as this?

Enter ARCHBISHOP OF CANTERBURY

ARCHBISHOP
God save thee, gentlemen.

MAYOR
O, thy Grace!

ARCHBISHOP
How fare thee, Leonard?

MAYOR
Thou art looking well, Michael.
We have ourselves in such a pickle here
What shall I do?

ARCHBISHOP
When these prodigies
Do so conjointly meet, let not men say
'These are their reasons; they are natural;'
For, I believe, they are portentous things
Unto the climate that they point upon.
Tis a sign from heaven, but cite me not.

MAYOR
Tis' very wise.
But must I sign a decree that all should pray?
Run to your houses! Fall upon your knees!

WINSTON
I be Winston, your Lordship. Employed withal these men
have I of late, but what visions have I seen that before my
God, I might not this believe without the sensible and true
avouch of mine own eyes. Things so terrible that each
particular hair on thy head 'twould stand on end, and turn thy
face a paler shade of white!

PETER
Well, thou could'st believe Master Pecker.

PECK
My name be Peck!

PETER
Or thou can resign yourself to the truth: that this city faces a
plague on a Biblical scale.

MAYOR
What mean you Biblical?

RAY
The wrath of Lord God, my liege.

Stars with trains of fire and dews of blood,
And Neptune's ocean like a cauldron boil.

EGON
Two score darkness will the face of Earth entomb.
The frame and huge foundation of the earth
Shall shake like a coward.

WINSTON
Spirits from the vasty deep will rise again!

PETER
Pagan sacrifice, cur and feline in unnatural bondship,
Hysterica passio!

MAYOR
Cease! Good sentences, and well pronounced.
And if thou art mistaken?

PETER
Take this from this if this be otherwise. And to the Tower we
shall go in peace. Yet if I be correct, and quelch this hellfire we
can, Lenny, thou wilt have saved the souls of many a
countrymen.

PECK
I shall not believe thou wilt be entreated to these men.

MAYOR
Remove him hence.

PETER
God save thee!

PECK
A plague pon you, Venkman, and a vengeance!
Time shall unfold what plighted cunning hides
Who covers faults at last with shame derides!

PETER
I shall send him baskets of fruit.

MAYOR
Come, shall we fall to work?

Exeunt.

SCENE 6

The streets of London. Music. Trumpets. Fanfare.
Soldiers escort the Ministers of Grace through the CROWD.

PETER
Friends, Londoners, Countrymen!

He raises RAY's hand high. Cheers from the CROWD.

Doctor Stantz! Would'st thou please?
A universal shout for he the heart of our band of brothers
here.
Thank ye. They adore thee. They most adore thee here!
Whatsoever my befall us gentles,
Stiffen the sinews, summon up the blood,
Disguise fair nature with hard-favored rage.

They look up. Lightning strikes.

RAY
Past the witching hour we may labor.

The earth quakes. The CROWD screams.
A pit opens below the Ministers. They fall in.
The earthquake suddenly stops. The crowd comes to its feet.

ENTER RAY from the pit, followed by the others.
CROWD cheers.

PETER
Very well. Tis' very well. They wish to be rough? We shall be
rough! And gentlemen cross England now abed
Shall think themselves accursed they were not here,
And hold their manhoods cheap whiles any speaks
That fought with us upon this Judgement day.

Exeunt.

An earthquake.

SCENE 7

Temple of Gozer. DANA and LOUIS stand on pedestals.
Lightning strikes. The gates open up.

Enter Minsters, exhausted.

RAY
Be this it?

PETER
Aye.

EGON
Gothic in its making. Finely made, I'faith.

RAY
To where doth yonder stair climb?

PETER
They ascend.

As they reach the top, lightning strikes DANA and LOUIS as they
turn into curs of terror.

PETER
Ay. She be a curtal dog. 'Tis all.

Enter GOZER.

RAY
'Tis a maid.

EGON
'Tis Gozer.

WINSTON

Methought Gozer be a man.

EGON
'Tis whatsoever it wish to be.

PETER
Whatsoever it be, it must breach our line!

RAY
Verily!

PETER
Have at her, Ray!

RAY steps forward

RAY
Gozer the Gozerian! Good ev'n to you! As deputy elect unto
the English crown and all his lands, I order thee forbear any
and all supernatural baseness and return forthwith to thy
place of origin!

PETER
Well said. Grammercie, cuz.

GOZER
Art thou a god?

RAY
Nay

GOZER
Then...death!

*She fires lightning at the four of them. They sail cross the temple,
clinging to the edge of the building. CROWD screams.*

WINSTON
Ray, if one should ask thou art a god, say thou but "Ay!"

PETER
Now under heavy judgment bears that life which this March-
chick deserves to lose.

PETER, RAY, EGON, WINSTON
Holding!

PETER
Heat your irons hot!

PETER, RAY, EGON, WINSTON
Smoking!

PETER
Make them hard!

PETER, RAY, EGON, WINSTON
Anon!

PETER
Let us show this ancient dissembling harlot how things be
done in Southwark.

They blast GOZER. She flips across the temple.

'Tis a nimble minx, is she not? Take aim upon the ground she
stands!

They blast again. GOZER vanishes.

PETER
Well, that task was easily met.

RAY
Into the air, and what seemed corporal
Melted, as breath into the wind!

WINSTON
Withal plentiful tools, our skills be sharp!

PETER
'Tis the time of the Miller!

EGON
In what particular thought to work I know not,
But in the gross and scope of mine opinion
This bodes some strange eruption to our state.

Earthquake. Rocks fall.

Look ye!

CROWD screams.

GOZER
Most needless creatures! Gozer the Gozerian, Gozer the
Destructor, Volguus Zildrohar, the Traveler, hast come!
Choose and perish!

RAY
What mean you choose? In faith we do not understand!

GOZER
Choose! Choose the form of the Destructor!

PETER
I have solved the demon's riddle most foul.
What'ere we set our minds to, thus is she.

If think we the Royal Inquisitor, then Royal Inquistor shall
appear and be the death of us and all held dear.
Make haste and clear thy pate.
And give as soft attachment to thy senses
As infants' empty of all thought!

GOZER
A drum, a drum!
The Traveler hath come.

PETER
Nay! Chose we not aught. Did thee make choice?

EGON
Nay!

PETER
Did'st thou?

WINSTON
A blank

PETER
I chose not aught!

They turn to RAY

RAY
'Twere by accident. It merely popped in.

PETER
What say you? What popped in?

RAY
To — To think upon...

Sounds of stomping and screaming.

EGON
Behold, lo, where it comes!

RAY
Nay! It cannot be!

WINSTON
What is it?

RAY
It cannot be!

WINSTON
Ray, what hast thou done?

RAY
It cannot be!

WINSTON
Oh, horrible, most horrible!

RAY
'Tis the Everlasting Puffed Man of Custard.

PETER
There be something that eyes see not each day.

RAY
Not a crime but a harmless remembrance.
Which in my childhood innocence I did dote upon;
A thing that could ne're bring us harm.
Master Everlasting Puffed…

PETER
Wise thoughts, cuz.

RAY
Many a time and oft hath we as children
Devoured such sweets withal powdered grins.

PETER
To bedlam with him, for he is grown mad. Egon, what think
thee?

EGON
Thy pardon, Venkman. I am bereft of all words.

WINSTON
Oh horrible!

Proper English Custard

Ingredients

570ml/1 pint milk
55ml/2fl oz single cream
1 vanilla pod or ½ tsp vanilla extract
4 eggs, yolks only
30g/1oz caster sugar
2 level tsp cornflour

Method

Bring the milk, cream and vanilla pod to simmering point slowly over a low heat.

Remove the vanilla pod (wash the vanilla pod, dry and store in jar with caster sugar to make vanilla sugar).

Whisk the yolks, sugar and cornflour together in a bowl until well blended

Pour the hot milk and cream on to the eggs and sugar, whisking all the time with a balloon whisk.

Return to the pan, (add vanilla extract if using) and over a low heat gently stir with a wooden spatula until thickened.

Pour the custard into a jug and serve at once.

To keep hot, stand the jug in a pan of hot water and cover the top with cling film to prevent skin forming.

Bells as Puffed-Man destroys a church.

PETER
You bucket of mother's pus!
Nary a soul, 'cept good King Harry
Shall in my towne lay waste an abbey !

RAY
O cursed slave! Roast him in sulphur!

They blast the Puffed Man. It sets him ablaze.
He begins to climb. They run and take cover

RAY
Tis such stuff as horrid dreams are made of:
Dealt death by a colossal custard man.

PETER
Ah, sirrahs, this unlooked-for sport comes well.
He be a sailor, he be in London;
Get he to a nunnery and all's well!

English Sailor as depicted by Cesare Vecellio, 1598-1600

EGON
A Most disobedient and refractory idea have I.
The gate doth swing both ways.
Reverse we could the evil through yonder gate
By the crossing of the streams.

PETER
Thy pardon, Egon. Thou said'st the crossing of streams was ill
favored.

RAY
The crossing of streams...

PETER
Thou wilt endanger our souls in this endeavor. Thou wilt
endanger our client, the Lady most pleasant who did pay us in
advance ere she came a dog.

EGON
Nary that. If we wrought out life, 'tis a hundred to one.

PETER
An admirable device! It pleases me to take part.

WINSTON
In faith, this task warrants double salary.

>   *Enter the Man of Custard. They flee to the temple.*

EGON
Make haste!

PETER
See thee on the shores of the undiscovered country, friend
Ray.

RAY
'Twas a pleasure, Doctor Venkman. The rest is labour, which
is not used for you.

They all Fire and cross the streams.

RAY, EGON, WINSTON
Crossing!

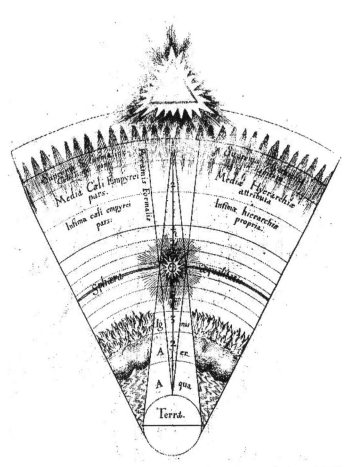

R. Fludd, Utriusque Cosmi, Vol. I, Oppenheim, 1617
(the Crossing of the Streams)

The four beams combine and blast into the temple.
The gates swing shut.

PETER, RAY, EGON, WINSTON cease firing.
The Temple of Gozer explodes. Master Custard does as well.

RAY
Winston, art thou well?

WINSTON
Ay, well.

RAY
Venkman? Spengler? Art thou well? Prithee, answer!

Enter EGON.

Oh, Spengler, art thou hurt?

EGON
I do feel like the floor of a carriage.

Enter PETER.

RAY
Good sir Peter?

PETER
Aye. Content.

RAY
Praise Jove. Thou art well, my friends?

EGON
Content.

RAY
And thee?

PETER
Content.

RAY
In sooth?

PETER
Aye.

RAY
I do smell the roasted hair of hound; at which my nose is in
great indignation.
O, I cry thy pardon, good sir Peter. Thy pardon. I did forget.

The statue begins to crumble. A hand emerges.

RAY
Behold!

The Ministers break ope the statue.

PETER
O, she's warm!
If this be magic, let it be an art
Lawful as eating.

EGON
She embraces him.

RAY
She hangs about his neck.
If she pertain to life, let her speak too.

Enter LOUIS with dog head.

LOUIS
Give me some light! Help! Give me some light!

PETER
Attend upon the dwarf!

LOUIS
What has befallen here?

DANA
What place is this? And all the skill I have
Remembers not these garments.
Oh, hello my Lord.

PETER
Do not infest your mind with beating on
The strangeness of this business. At picked leisure
Which shall be shortly, single I'll resolve you –
Which to you shall seem probable – of every
These happened accidents. Till when, be cheerful.

EGON
He is well.

LOUIS
The landlord will be drunk with cholar.

RAY
Art thou well, good sir?

LOUIS
Who be ye?

RAY
We be the Ministers of Grace.

LOUIS
Who keeps thy books?

RAY
Good Sir Tully, thou art most fortunate and must give thanks
you have lived so long.

LOUIS
In faith, I know it truly.

RAY
Thou hast born witness to the grandest tear betwixt the
firmament and earth ere the fiery days of Kent when warlike
dragons reigned terror from above.

LOUIS
Cheered each part!

EGON
We would desire a fragment of thy brain matter.

LOUIS
All the same

Exit all but WINSTON

EPILOGUE

WINSTON
Pete and Dana were not wed
Someone else would take her bed
The child Oscar that she bore
Would prove an ev'n bigger chore
Of living paintings, statues too
But let's return 'tween me and you
If we spirits have offended
Think on this and all is mended
That you have but slumbered here
Whilst these visions did appear
So dream on custard, and do not frown
For how could you not love this towne?
And clap thy hands if we be friends
For Winston shall restore amends.

He Exits.

THE END

AFTERWORD

For the Elizabethan audience, ghosts were part of the world they lived in.

The spirit world and the human world were permeable.

~ Justin Champion, British historian

In the spring of 2010 I was in a production of Richard II at a tiny 45 seat theatre in North Hollywood, California. During a rehearsal one evening, a fellow cast member handed me his iphone3 and asked, "Have you seen this yet?" What I saw on the glowing screen changed my life. It was an adaptation of the 1994 film *Pulp Fiction* rewritten in the language of Shakespeare. Numerous contributors from all over the country had chosen a scene or scenes to adapt, and had posted it in this message board. The result was an incomplete but incredibly funny version of Tarantino's film.

Up until this time, the only adaptations I had seen of Shakespeare were in how individual directors had decided to set the plays – *King Lear* in an insane asylum, or *Twelfth Night* in an 80's nightclub. But this was something new. This was parody. Jules and Vince were still two murderous hitmen, but now carried daggers and spoke in iambic pentameter.

I knew right away that I needed to be part of this. I filled in the missing scenes, held auditions, and in the summer of 2011, "Pulp Shakespeare" premiered at the Hollywood Fringe Festival. It was an instant hit and the first show for my fledgling theatre company "Her Majesty's Secret Players".

I was now on the hunt for my next show. By now, Shakespearean mashups were becoming more common: Notable are *Two Gentlemen of Lebowski* by Adam Bertocci (Simon and Schuster 2010), and *William Shakespeare's STAR WARS* by Ian Doescher (QuirkBooks 2013); there were even Shakespearean adaptations of *The Godfather* and *Breaking Bad.*

But as enjoyable as it would have been to direct those plays, I wanted to adapt my own. And it had to be personal. What movie not only spoke to me but was well known enough to large numbers of people? There was only one choice: Ivan Reitman's 1984 hit comedy, *Ghostbusters.*

In 1988 I was in the third grade and the founding member of a Ghostbusters club. We wore cardboard proton packs and carried cardboard traps and would bravely descend into the dark basements of neighboring houses in search of pesky spirits. "How will you get the ghosts into the Kleenex boxes?" my brother would sarcastically ask. My answer was to "lure them with candy."

By college, I was not only studying and performing Shakespeare, but was in a legitimate paranormal research group (if such a thing exists). My cardboard equipment had now been upgraded with EMF recorders, temperature readers and digital cameras. We recorded ghostly voices and even "full form vaporous apparitions," to quote Ray Stantz.

But I didn't need to be convinced that the spirit world existed. I held strong to that belief from a young age. I grew up in New England, where ghost stories were popular at the dinner table. What interested me now was spirituality in Elizabethan England. With the average person's lifespan only thirty-five years, death was always around the next corner. It was no surprise then that the Elizabethans were a superstitious lot, executing men and women for witchcraft years before the first Puritan stepped foot in Massachusetts.

However, according to John Mullan, Professor of English at University College London, *"devout Protestants did not believe in ghosts, and Protestant theologians often argued that apparitions could therefore only be devices of the Devil to disturb and mislead Christians."* Prince Hamlet, for example, does not take the words of the ghost at face value, and stages 'The Mousetrap' for stronger proof of his Uncle's guilt.

Mullan continues that, *"for Roman Catholics, there was another possibility, for they believed in Purgatory, a state of moderated torment in which a soul would undergo purification before entering Heaven and could benefit from the prayers of the living. There is much evidence that many individual Protestants, though supposedly scorning the idea of Purgatory, did believe in ghosts, and that popular superstition did not accord with Church doctrine."*

We know that Shakespeare included ghosts in five of his plays, often as portents of pertinent information. In that respect, someone "busting" a ghost that is simply trying to relay a message or perform some deed left undone in life would seem very counterproductive. Then again, Venkman does try to communicate with the library ghost at the beginning of the film, and she is not in the mood to chat.

How then did the public receive these supernatural characters on the stage? Michael Dobson, Director of the Shakespearean Institute in Birmingham, explains:

"The theatre can be the place you go to look into the next world, a threshold between this world and the next and it can represent spirits, ghosts, deities. Or it can be just the place you can go to see the world the way it is; to show human behavior that is secular and rational."

As for parapsychology in Tudor England, the scientists or "philosophers" of Shakespeare's time were busier in their attempts to turn raw metal into gold, or gazing at the night sky. There are two references to an exorcist in the plays, one in *All's Well That Ends Well* and another in *Julius Caesar*, but the term meant one who calls up spirits rather than one who sends them back to hell as in Roy Blatty's 1976 film. Queen Elizabeth the First even had a magician/occult philosopher/alchemist in her court by the name of John Dee (1527 – 1608). It has been said that in addition to performing experiments before the Queen, tutoring members of the court, and offering astrological advice, Dee recorded hundreds of spirit conversations, which he believed to be from angels.

Still, despite the differences, there are many similarities between the plays of William Shakespeare and the 1984 film. For one, there are apocalyptic passages in Shakespeare that closely mirror dialogue from *Ghostbusters*, end of the world prophecies of the stars falling or the dead rising from their graves to walk the earth. In Act 5, scene 1, Ray and Winston are quoting the Book of Revelation. Such text could have been lifted directly from the pages of *Hamlet* or *Macbeth*. It is no surprise then that Shakespeare's later plays were written during the reign of James I, whose revised Bible (translated in English) was completed in 1611. To say William Shakespeare was influenced by religion is an understatement. There are more references to the Bible in his plays than any other Elizabethan playwright's, roughly 1,200.

The dialogue between Dana Barrett and Peter Venkman in the film, while not apocalyptic, is similar to the witty banter between Beatrice and Benedick in Much Ado About Nothing. They tease and insult one another but somehow end up together in the end. Then there is the character of Louis Tully who very much plays the fool or clown, someone for the audience to laugh at in between the scary scenes. Peter also plays a witty fool, much like Bottom in A Midsummer Night's Dream or Feste in Twelfth Night, while Slimer is definitely a Falstaff or Sir Toby Belch type, the drunken fool.

It was in finding similarities like these that made writing this adaptation so enjoyable. In the year 2014 the world celebrated the 450th anniversary of Shakespeare's birth. Oddly enough, it was also the 30th anniversary of *Ghostbusters*. Coincidence? Maybe. I for one am happy that both have endured and will continue to delight audiences for generations to come until cats and dogs are living together...okay, maybe cats and giant Sloars.

Gozer speaks. From left to right: Jordan Monsell, Drew Doyle, Alex Knox, and Dan White. Photo by Rich Clark Photography

ACKNOWLEDGEMENTS

I would first and foremost like to thank my talented cast of the original stage reading of *Ministers of Grace* : Drew Doyle, Dan White, Libby Letlow, Alex Knox, Patrick Wenk-Wolff, Paul Willson, and Paul Reese. Plays are meant to be performed and you guys brought the house down!

My editors Ruth Monsell and Roy Sonobel.

The generous individuals who backed my Kickstarter campaign:
Jacob Phillip Shaw, Danilo Sanchez Jr., Douglas Lanier, Tayo Kaufman, George and Priscilla Cunningham Candice Colbert, Shawn Carlow, Michael Holmes, Josefine Klemm, John H Longmaid, Sam McClellan, Steven Alloway, Veronica Wilson, Claire Cashin, Martin Jago Dana Pollak, Clockwork Couture, Marcy Mahoney, The Pollak Family, Tamara Jones, Neil Sheehan, Scott Douglas Hallie Smith, Diani&Devine, Matthew DeCapua, Geoff Dunaway, C. Frost, Christopher Newell, Jay Potter, Susan Schullery, Sandra, Jannine Puglia Gaudet, Matt Ritchey, and Alex Knox.

Dan Aykroyd and Ellen Dostal for their kind reviews.

I'd also like to thank Evelyn Torres, the Bearded Lady Mystic Museum, The Hollywood Fringe Festival, David Carradine, Robin Groves, Marcia Neumeier, and all my Shakespeare professors over the years. Thank you for your inspiration and insight!

ABOUT THE AUTHOR

Jordan Monsell is a freelance writer and illustrator working in the little hamlet that is Los Angeles. He is a graduate of the University of Connecticut's theatre program with a minor in paranormal studies.

Ministers of Grace is his first book. Visit him on the interwebs at www.jordanmonsell.com

Made in the USA
Middletown, DE
31 December 2019